T0024919

RELIGION
or
RELIGWRONG

Everald "Gosple Fish" Thomas

authorHOUSE®

AuthorHouse™ UK
1663 Liberty Drive
Bloomington, IN 47403 USA
www.authorhouse.co.uk
Phone: 0800.197.4150

© 2019 Everald "Gosple Fish" Thomas. All rights reserved.

No part of this book may be reproduced, stored in a retrieval system, or
transmitted by any means without the written permission of the author.

Scriptures marked KJV are taken from the KING
JAMES VERSION (KJV): KING JAMES
VERSION, public domain.

Published by AuthorHouse 02/05/2019

ISBN: 978-1-7283-8425-2 (sc)
ISBN: 978-1-7283-8426-9 (e)

Print information available on the last page.

Any people depicted in stock imagery provided by Getty Images are models,
and such images are being used for illustrative purposes only.
Certain stock imagery © Getty Images.

This book is printed on acid-free paper.

Because of the dynamic nature of the Internet, any web addresses or
links contained in this book may have changed since publication and
may no longer be valid. The views expressed in this work are solely those
of the author and do not necessarily reflect the views of the publisher,
and the publisher hereby disclaims any responsibility for them.

The Bible
-The Truth and the Lie-

*It is good to **note** that within all of this, in the end, we may never know; but all we are craving is to listen to the voice of "Truth". I am willing to change my mind if the "evidence" emerges.*

ACKNOWLEDGEMENT

Writing a book is definitely more challenging than I have imagined, but really prove to be more compensating than I could have ever predicted.

I have to start by thanking my remarkable wife Sonia, from the proof-reading of each chapter, to the advice on selecting the type of look I had wanted for the cover, and the constant reminder most of the nights that I need to pause and go rest my eyes and my pan-fried brain from all the writing and researching, as there's another day called "tomorrow." For this, I am eternally grateful for your never-ending kind support!

I also want to thank my daughter Meisha who continues to pose challenging questions about religion and spirituality, where I have been forced to go sometimes beyond the surfaces and rock my brain to bring her honest, valid and factual answers.

Also some of my very good long-standing friends like Clive Baxter, Mr Newland "Culture Rebel" and Rohan "Baya" Percells who forever actively maintained their strong religious views, especially Mr Baxter who always tried to wind me up with his undying love for Jesus.

Special thanks to Vincent "Daddy Boom" Rose, General TK and Jimmy Crazy, Kevin and Akhenaton for their ceaseless support.

I want to thank my daughters Shola and Sadie; my two lovely sons Damian and Samuel who have always expressed their ultimate faith in everything I undertake. It is really nice to have kind-supportive picknies.

Very special thanks extended to my youngest daughter Junelle "Sandy" who has always been defiant with the religious dogma, and regularly put me on the spot to prove my stance.

I also want to thank her, as well as my good-hearted nephew Jovel and wonderful Sharlene, who took time from their busy schedules and went out of their way to capture and organize those beautiful pictures which we used for the book.

You have all contributed immensely and I am forever indebted to your dedicated support.

I would like to also give a special thank you to my cousin Michelle Stephenson and mummy Patsy, who unwittingly were not aware that the idea to begin writing this book occurred the day after we attended mummy P's wedding.

We all sat in the kitchen on the evening of the reception, joking, laughing and having a great time, when the inevitable topic of the fieriest debate on the subject of RELIGION, exploded.

I even remember someone shouted from the other room, asking if we could close the door (Lol).

Thankfully, the night ended with everyone still talking to each other and smiling, and the debate inspired the initiation of this manuscript.

I want to thank all of you who were a part of that debate for being an inspiration!

Very importantly and with extremely high regards, I want to thank and bless a few people who have inspired me through their teachings for numerous years; some which are now passed on to spirit.

Teachers and mentors like Mutabaruka, Maya Angelou, Dr Ray Hagins, Jane Elliott, Bob Marley, Rosa Louise Parks, Dr John Henrik Clarke, Bishop John Spong, Mary Seacole, Dalai Lama, Marcus Garvey and Louis Farrakhan just to name a few.

Finally, I want to thank the Author House publishing team, who has been nothing other than a guiding light in every step of the journey, in bringing this book into your hands today.

I want to first thank my publishing consultant Lara Fauna who politely and professionally explained the entire spectrum of my publishing from start to finish, including my rights, what to do and what to expect from my contract with Author House. You have been a reliable source of delegation, and this includes May Arado, Carlo, the panel from the ALC and the entire Author House team of professionals. Thank you all for being my pilot throughout this journey.

Follow the story of when the Truth and the Lie went swimming...

As it was told; one day the Truth and the Lie decided to go for a swim, so they went to the beach nearby. As they stood by the water, the Lie said to the Truth, "Let's see who can dive underneath the water and stay the longest." So the Truth went in and put his head down and began diving.

Suddenly the Lie decided to get cunning, so he picked up the Truth's clothes, put them on, and ran off down the road. The Truth happened to emerge from the water just in time to see the Lie running away in his clothes, so he got out of the water and chased him. As he chased him down the road, a group of people saw the Lie flash by in the Truth's clothes and said, "Hey! That looks like the Truth." _Moments later, the Truth rushed passed with no clothes on, so someone shouted, "Hey! This looks like the naked Truth!"

The Truth eventually caught up with the Lie, **uncovered** him and took his clothes back.

– (*Credit to Bishop Ray Hagins*)

CHAPTER 1

The Primary Age. – *It began at the cradle!*

I was only eleven when I started reading the Bible, and it was because my father and some of his friends who he used to hang out with who triggered the spark and motivated me to read it. There was Mr Pepper and Pepsi, who were brothers; and another friend called Ras High-Eye who played the drums. They all love the Bible and believe that demons are flying everywhere.

Daddy frequently called me, to come and read him a psalm or two, as he was a non-reader. He somehow remembered a wealth of ancestral wisdom and sayings. He would say when referring to the Bible, "if you follow the **Good Book** you will never go wrong".

Daddy and Mommy were kind of old skool Bible parents, even though they weren't practising on any religious level. They probably went to church once or twice a year, if lucky: but they made sure they sent us every Sunday.

I got glued to the book and fell in love with it, so I read it almost every day. By the time I reached 15, I was a full-blown preacher in my local community church.

I grew up in a little village called Thompson Pen of Spanish Town, in southeast central Jamaica, in the parish of St. Catherine.

Surrounded by numerous churches in the district, roughly 14-18 churches per square mile, it became very easy for me as a result to fit in. I explored and probed Christianity and quickly became a prominent figure within the church community. I was later tagged with the name "Gospel Fish, aka the Mighty Reverend."

I spent near to 4 years in the church searching and preaching the scriptures. I was a very committed Christian and I **full**-joyed my little young self in the flock. I learned to play instruments such as the drums, rhythm and bass guitar and percussion. I had a good innings, I must say; and was very honoured to be called Brother Thomas as a teenager.

I was always inquisitive and desirous for information. I love to know the truth. I was never a fan of lies. I told the odd small ones to my wife now and then, but hardly got away with it. I have never been a good fibber.

More and more, day by day, things etched in my brain, which were either too confusing or didn't make much sense within the context of the scriptures. Pretty soon, I couldn't help but questioning my uncertainties. I put almost everything I once confidently preached, under the lens of a microscope. As I did that, my Christian life started to disintegrate, and it soon came to an abrupt end.

I began spotting contradictions, from the beginning of the creation story in Genesis 1 and 2.

I questioned the killings of children ordered by God in the Bible *-2 Kings 2:- 23-24*, *Deuteronomy 21:- 18-21* and many more. I also questioned the permission of the buying and trading of slaves in *Exodus 21* and *Leviticus 25*, and it even carried on over to the New Testament *-Luke 12:- 47-48*, *Ephesians 6:- 5,* and *Timothy 6:- 1-2*.

I realised that something didn't quite add up here. One of the most appalling and disgusting text I have read in the Bible, is in Numbers chapter 31:- 13-18, when Moses instructed his officers and captains to kill all the women who had committed trespass against the Lord, and specifically those women who had slept with men. But they should keep the virgins alive for themselves.

What God would inspire these words in a holy scripture?

This book is infused with contradictions from the beginning right to the last chapter, and we will definitely examine some of these more closely later on.

Chapter 2

Spirituality vs Religion –*Let's take a look!*

There's an old saying "Religion is for people who are afraid of going to hell: Spirituality is for people who have already been there."

For many people spirituality and religion are the same. They see no difference; they're convinced that they walk hand in hand.

But they are remarkably different, and the confusing thing about these two is that they are tied to the same fundamental divine spark. They are diametrically opposed in that one of them goes through a third party to access this divine spark, while the other uses a direct connection to the same central source.

"Any religious person can be spiritual, but no spiritual person needs religion." I didn't quite understand what this quote meant the first time I heard it, because I remained steadfast, clenching to what I believe.

However, I was deeply concerned about understanding this religious reality, which is why I digressed into the woods searching for answers; searching for **Truth**.

As I began to delve into the historical layers, I found that religion is basically a system of doctrines documented and dictated in a book and preached back to you. The book then becomes the principal power of control. Its concepts purely derived from ancient human ideology. One could say that the original purpose of its intent, was to cautiously guide and control the behaviour of the masses, as man tried to understand the cosmos and the whole concept of how the universe worked and came into being. This was a long way before man stumbled upon science.

And so, the structure of religion refers to an external form rather than an internal form. It's an organised belief system, which is based on cultural traditions, customs, and ritualistic practices. Each belief system is centred on a deity; like a Buddha, a Jesus, or a Mohammed etc.

Religion becomes a label that was invented by man. But God is not religious. God is not a Muslim, a Christian nor a Buddhist. God is that source of universal energy accessed from within.

Spirituality, on the other hand, is internal. It is personal; each individual is born with it. The essence of spirituality is about personal growth and development on all levels. Every single human being is born with spirituality. You don't need another person to dictate this to you from a book. Every person was conceived as a spiritual being by the law of the universe. Sleep state, dreams and meditations are all doors to the spirit world.

Spirituality is a universal consciousness. It promotes love, understanding, empathy and purification of the mind. It also shows that we are all interconnected no matter where we are. It allows people to take personal responsibility and awaken their abilities.

Spirituality elevates individuals in their journeys of self, which holds paramount importance in life. It is not something that one can practise; it is intuition. It is **who you are.**

CHAPTER 3

How Did The Lie Become The Truth.? - *Let's examine it!*

The more it opens up, the more I am seeing the danger of the mental damage this is causing in our minds. The injection of words, pictures and stories into our brains over a period of time, begin to form a permanent **programming**, which we eventually accept as "the truth". It becomes more convincing naturally, when we see people of influence, such as doctors, theologians, lawyers, historians, archaeologists; accepting it through the same channel. All having the same religious mind-set and giving credence to the same notion. Ultimately, this impression becomes implanted in our psyche and therefore helped to make it look even more factual and real in our mental paradigm.

I remember saying to my wife, after reading Genesis 3 from the King James Version, "I really don't know how all these years I had believed that a snake actually spoke to a person."

Looking back now, I am certain that believing this is a mental disorder.!! Religion does this to you.

<u>Let's examine some of these texts.</u>

Bearing in mind, that God is omnipotent, omniscient and omnipresent. The God who is all POWERFUL!

How could God even have an adversary? Who in a reasonably <u>sane</u> state of mind would want to **oppose** God?

Aside from certain branches of science, atheism, and other sects, that definitely oppose the God theory, I want to speak particularly from the platform of spirituality and religion.

I find that questions related to the Bible, when analysed and put forward, tend to always get a supernatural explanation from religious supporters.

We were told that God created this adversary called Satan. Throughout these thousands of years, this "dude" Satan has been hammered for every bad thing that happened on this planet. He keeps doing the extreme opposite of everything that God represents. The explanation we get is that God deliberately put Satan in that position, exactly where he is, to make war against everything that God stands for.

Isaiah 45:- 7 says, *"I form the light, and create darkness: I make peace, and create evil: I the Lord do all these things."* <u>How</u> -? <u>Why</u> -?

I thought that God hated evil. We were told that God brutally destroyed people who associate themselves with evil. We learned all this from the pages of the scriptures.

Read how it echoes in **Deuteronomy 4:- 24-26**; *"For the Lord thy God is a consuming fire, even a jealous God. When thou shalt beget children, and children's children, and ye shall have remained long in the land, and shall corrupt yourselves, and make a graven image, or the likeness of any thing, and shall do EVIL in the sight of the Lord thy God, to provoke him to anger: I call heaven and earth to witness against you this day, that ye shall soon utterly perish from off the land whereunto ye go over Jordan to possess it; ye shall not prolong your days upon it, but shall utterly be destroyed."*

Can you see what it is doing to your mental state? It eventually changes your personality. And it gets worse when you become a convert and you attempt to try and justify what it means, even though you don't really believe what you are saying, but you feel that you have to say it.

This is where it becomes worrying for me, as it puts you in a compromised position of brainwashed and self-deception. What this shows, is that Religion tends to outline clear and strict rules of what God want and doesn't want; but in the same gulp of breath, it is making out like God is an idiot.

For instance, preachers and most biblical scholars have told us exclusively that Moses wrote the first 5 books of the Old Testament, and every bit of the scriptures are inspired by God. How could Moses then explain in **Deuteronomy**, which is supposedly his 5th book written by him, and tells us in great detail how he died and buried?

Here is how it reads in chapter 34 verses 5-6, (written in the third person perspective). *"So Moses the servant of the*

Lord died there in the land of Moab, according to the word of the Lord. And he buried him in a valley in the land of Moab, over against Bethpeor: but no man knoweth of his sepulchre unto this day."

All I can say, if Moses really wrote that, he has to be undoubtedly the **greatest** writer ever to have walked the earth, for him to write about his own death, detailing how he died and was buried. **Wow!**

Here is another one you can put in your imaginary pipe and pull on it.!

In the creation story of Genesis, God gets angry with man starting in chapter 3 and went on threatening to kill them all in chapter 6, saving only Noah and his family. Apparently man became wicked and corrupt in his heart according to **Genesis 6:- 6-7**. Here is what the text reads;

"And it repented the Lord that he had made man on the earth, and it grieved him at his heart. And the Lord said, I will destroy man whom I have created from the face of the earth; both man, and beast, and the creeping thing, and the fowls of the air; for it repenteth me that I have made them."

Now, my natural thinking brain, led me to ask, "**What sin did the animals commit**" -? The cows, the camels, the grasshoppers and the flying eagle, why did they have to get killed -? What mood was God in?

It just leaves me wondering if God is **<u>Bipolar</u>**?

CHAPTER 4

------- ·◆·◆·◆·◆· -------

<u>DEAR PASTOR!</u> - *Can I get a Amen*

We live in a logical universe where our lives are based on the principle of rational thinking. We face real life issues everyday. We live in reality, and we don't live our lives in our mind. The present moment is a continuum and is always active doing its random U-turns. Sometimes slapping us where it hurts. And when it does, peril threatens our future.

So this is the world to which we are now exposed. And when it travels from "**the loo to the fan**," our safest approach is to always be pragmatic and sensible.

This is when we need workable methods and decisions and not mysterious or pathetic answers, like what the church is off loading today.

If I put my foot in the pastor's flip-flops, having the understanding of my role being firmly grounded on the bedrock of religion, I would be minded to asked myself from time to time, how practical is it really, in todays society, to listen to some of Jesus's most comforting words and really put them into action.

For instance Jesus says, "*Come unto me, all ye that labour and are heavy laden and I will give you rest*"; **Matthew 11:28.**

Real sweet and reassuring, but in all honesty, how functional is that in todays 2019, 21st century reality?

Realistically, we cannot drop our responsible working methods that we have established to cope with life, by just getting baptised and following Jesus, and genuinely expect it to be a Lottery win from that point onwards.

That's blatantly a deception!

I can assure you, these ancient **myths** currently have a disabled relationship with today's reality.

The bible presents a lot of profound and startling instructions from God that doesn't work. Faith maybe good, especially when you're inspired, but blind faith is destructive. It's really you, just burying your head in the "*no where*," having no GPS or map about your life, and simply hoping that things will go in your favour. Throwing yourself into blind faith rather than searching the facts, soon let you find yourself fearing, when there is nothing even there to fear.

And yes you should follow your heart, but take your brain with you.

And since we were not born with that biblical magic wand, we should probably just use our brain App.

Getting the fish hooked!

I read the bible over and over; I was in love with it. I was under its **spell**.! Even when there were obvious pressing questions, I couldn't ask them because of my spell bounded mind that kept telling me to have faith and trust God's word. It has always been a constant wrestling between the soulful reality and that other part of your brain.

I kept wondering, how are the churches applying their pre-existing religious ethics in today's logical world, without breaking or tarnishing any of their sacred covenants?

The pastors are the primary leaders of the flock!

Given, you are someone who holds, what you call a divine licence, as God's agent; your claim is that you take God's word around to the people.

That's a very high stool you sit on, and even though in my view it is ***fake power***, you're extremely influential with it. Your responsibility is **huge**! Not to be taken lightly, especially what people become from the magnitude of your preaching.

Probably no one would have ever taken any notice or even bothered to follow the scriptures, if you were not there to hammer it in their brain; and the alarming thing is, you manage to get them to pay you to do it as well.

<u>What lessons can we take from our religious community!</u>

I'm honestly not sure if there's any! The religious community are stubborn, and they have been this way for ages. It is even worse now that it has grown into a multi-billion-merchandise profession; it's a business now, and mankind being mixed with money is a very bad combination. They are the two worse kinds!

Many preachers all over the globe are now carrying licensed guns because they have to protect their assets. It doesn't seem like this "faith in God alone" business, is enough to protect them anymore. What message are they then sending out to those they are preaching the word to?

Again, I ask in humble terms, how far do you intend to take this **Lie,** Dear Pastor; handing it down to generation after generation. I trust you sleep well in your bed at night with integrity. Amen!

CHAPTER 5

THE HOLY DRUG! - *Is religion a drug.?*

Well it makes people fall in love with it so deep that they place it above **everything** including family, friends and there closest loved ones. If there are any critics out there who are attempting to uphold different views, they will be dismissed and shut down instantly, without even a pinprick of second thought. And I know, because I was serving on that stage. It gives you this kind of "fictitious power" above non-religious people who don't see your point of view.

The false feeling we get, is as if you and God are "exceptionally" close buddies; and more so because he is the **boss**! So therefore in order to stand out differently from the rest and claim divine rights to this passion, the church followers exclusively name themselves "The Children of God" and all other humans are called "Sinners".

This is hard Drugs! This sentiment swims around in your thoughts everyday; it stays in your brain and in your heart. It even makes you say stupid things and defend it; like God says to "kill your son, by stoning him to death in front of

the village if he's disobedient." ***Deuteronomy 21: 18-21***.
"**What**" -?

This is a serious "**Holy**" drug! I have seen this drug in action countless times. For some people it takes them down to the ground and they roll themselves on the floor, speaking in tongues which of course they themselves haven't got the faintest clue to begin to understand what it is they are saying from their own mouths. They just blindly open up to this channel and allow themselves to fantasize with what has been preached to them, as they believe that this is what God wants.

Come on! Get up off the floor and pull yourself together; you don't need to display a performance to express to God that you're obeying the rules.

We first heard of this strange spirit filled performance in **Acts 2** from verse 1:

"And when the day of Pentecost was fully come, they were all with one accord in one place. And suddenly there came a sound from heaven as of a rushing mighty wind, and it filled all the house where they were sitting. And there appeared unto them cloven tongues like as of fire, and it sat upon each of them. And they were all filled with the Holy Ghost, and began to speak with other tongues, as the Spirit gave them utterance."

The "Holy Drug" Test – You may require a needle

Now hear a bit of the scientific viewpoint on this. The neuroscientists centre in Utah did some studies of the brain on a group of religious individuals, relying on the MRI scans to determine what happens in the human brain when someone is highly religious. The researchers from the University found that a religious experience can be just as addictive as **love** or as using **drugs.** According to Dr Michael Ferguson's report, they activated what is known as The Reward Circuits in the brain, similar to a drug-induced euphoric state.

Luckily for me, I myself never got so much of the "Holy drug" poison, but I still got infected; and I managed to poison a lot of people sadly, by presenting them the drug in my evangelisation.

One of the sensible Bible passage!

Now on the flip side, here is where the church behaves normal and morally decent-*ish*. I read **Galatians 5: 22-23** and it says *"But the fruit of the Spirit is love, joy, peace, longsuffering, gentleness, goodness, faith, Meekness, temperance: against such there is no law".*

I could easily work with the fruit of this kind of spirit. This would be more in the form of a Meditation for me; sitting quietly and filling up my inner self with the spirit of Love, Joy, Peace, Long suffering, goodness, faith, meekness. - Not sure about "temperance" in the biblical sense, cause I love my odd glass of red wine and dragon stout now and again.

And being a person, who has never got drunk in my life, I can simply nod my head to **Ephesians 5: 18-19**, that says *"And be not drunk with wine, wherein is excess; but be filled with the Spirit; Speaking to yourselves in psalms and hymns and spiritual songs, singing and making melody in your heart to the Lord."*

All this I can handle reasonably on a spiritual platter. These are all tools of connecting internally with the divine.

Changes felt!

Now in saying this, we can see that there is a significant change of attitudes in many Christians outlook today, especially when it comes to comparing the version of the Old and the New Testaments scriptures.

For instance if you hit on any derogatory passage from the Old Testament, say like, God ordered the killing of all the first born in Egypt including the killing of all firstborn cattle under Moses; **(Exodus 12)** Some of them have this kind of way to sway you, to let you know that the Old Testament is somewhat expired and doesn›t quite fit in todays world. But when it comes to the New Testament and Jesus "The Christ", all cards are off the table. This is where it gets interesting. -Welcome to the **fireworks**!

It is not so bad to view the Old Testament as metaphoric according to some religious people; compromise is already put in place. But touching the New Testament and its supernatural tenets, like the virgin birth, raising of the dead and walking on water! They'll tell you straight up that all of those things did happen, and none of it is metaphorical!

I asked a Jesus friend of mine the other day, **when was Jesus born?** He said Jesus was born in the winter, around the year 1 AD. I reminded him that according to the scripture in Matthew chapter 2, King Herod wanted to kill the baby Jesus when he was born. But as the history books confirm,

King Herod was born 74 BC and died 4 BC in Jericho, so how could he have wanted to kill Jesus when he died before Jesus was born?

All of this is just laughable when you listen to it. It's like we are really saying God is not so great and omnipotent after all, and I completely disagree with that.

You get the feeling when you read some of the scriptures, that God wasn't quite sure of a lot of what **he** done at the beginning, and as time went by **he** adjusted it accordingly!

He made man in Genesis, but then decided after a while that they are not what he had expected; so he killed them all and restarted the planet again with a small family of eight. He allowed these new residents to replenish back the earth; but somehow it happened again, it still wasn't working out with man as far as God was concerned.

So according to the texts, God came up with an even more sinister plan to destroy man, using fire this time which is the notion of the Burning Hell; the ultimate afterlife location.

Is God even capable of making these bad errors of judgement and writing them down? Can they hear how ridiculous this is sounding? I wouldn't swallow that tablet, not even with two spoons of honey!

And that is why it is difficult for most people to take the bible as the dictated word of God.

CHAPTER 6

<u>INTELLIGENT BULLYING</u> - *Religious style!*

Only if we just live as part of, and adopt the pace of nature, blending harmoniously with the species and the landscape, and just breathe in the natural art of God.

But we can't live like this without getting told of what God wants us to do, and **not** to do, by someone who was just born the other day. Someone who is always claiming knowledge of God, but can't substantiate, and they lay burdensome responsibilities and demands upon humanity's free intelligence and sound thinking; and I suppose they think that God should be flattered!

These people profess that they have a sophisticated understanding of God, and they are ready to download it on to your hardrive if you just open your mouth to yawn.

Sometimes the way they approach you, it feels like someone simply wants to stick you up and rob you of your mind, - and you dare not say a word on top of it.

Basically they are saying, *"I **don't** eat strawberries, so you **shouldn't** eat them either."*

How can they not see that this is a kind of "Holy Writ" dictatorship!

Most of the time, their approach feels like harassment, and of course when you object to it, the feeling of prejudice and bigotry start setting in.

To be fair, it can be very wounding to your intellectual principles, when they're telling you everything what Jesus did and said; saying it with the impression that they were standing right there at the foot of the cross when he was crucified.

I am a strong supporter of the God thesis than any other universal claim out there.

And one of my main reason is, I still haven't heard one rational explanation that gives me reasonable cause to believe that there is <u>not</u> a God source or divine intelligence, operating behind this perfectly fine-tuned arrangement.

Everything balanced in melody, working in total unison, harmonizing perfectly on the bed of nature.

The wise teacher Lao Tzu once said, *"Nature does not hurry, yet everything is accomplished,"* and this means that the universe is consciously tailored to support life.

But here's the thing; believing that there is a Divine God is one thing, and pulling someone to one side, to black or white-mail them saying, "Mate here is God! He laid out his rules to a few men over 2000 years ago and you will need to follow these commandments, or he will get angry and punish you very bad later when you die, or give you Cancer and Dementia while you live." These are two very different things. The latter is intimidating!

We should be able to live and mingle together, without others forcing doctrinal or religious viewpoint upon anyone. We're exactly of the same made up components, except some are more dishonest than others. But no one is better than anyone in anatomy and physiology!

The great Bob Marley once said, *"When the rain falls, it doesn't fall on one man's house top."* So no one is exceptional, we are all the same, and you were not here two- thousand years ago. You're just searching for the truth just like me.

Things would be so much easier if you could just ***show us the proof***!

Stop telling us the biblical accounts over and over. Start showing us some "impossible-to-deny" evidence, and I am sure many of us would view religion in a completely new light. All you are required to do is to prove your contentions.

There are so many people that have been mis-directed from their own spirituality and become confused. They started following other cultures philosophy and got lost. Nothing can be more devastating to a person than finding out that you have been conned, misled or lied to.

It destroys all elements of trust between you and that deluder. And when it hits you really hard, it leaves a blueprint right in the middle of your heart. - Stop the Religious **Bullying!** It's not consoling anyone.

CHAPTER 7

<u>WHO AM I - WHY AM I HERE</u> - *Two BIG Perplexities*

Yes, very thought provoking questions, and who or what know the real answers, still isn't clear. We cannot help but probe our minds everyday into this mystification, because one thing for certain is that life really matters!

We being here, is not an illusion.

The procreation for human beings is one of life's greatest miracles and none of us came here by accident. Sex maybe popular, but creating a baby can be very tricky! (lol)

The instructions sent for building our bodies inside the womb, and the complicated process that leads to the human life being born is, divinely remarkable.

As for outside the womb, the universal settings matched perfectly with life form. Humans and animals, and everything existing are raised within this home. You have to say the design and model of this home was skilfully and intentionally carved to accommodate us. Is it just a matter of meaningful coincidence -?

Everything is here ready for us to use. Food just pops up from out the ground and so does our medicine when we get ill.
All the tools we need to shape and enhance our life are within reach.
The place is well kitted out with every material.
Nothing that you will ever need is outside.
So it looks like I was suppose to be here.

You know they say, ***"Change the way you look at things; and the things you look at change."***

Well I've been doing that a lot, trying to breathe oxygen into the puzzling "who am I, why am I here" question.

But knowing that knowledge is infinite is the reason I have never put a lock or a cap on it.

Always open to welcome new information, because when knowledge comes, then comes change. You just can't be the same person armed with new knowledge!

We are definitely important to life; and I am aware, as well as hold the conviction of a **Divine Force** working behind the scene of our astonishing well-organised universe.

Call it God! Call it Allah! Call it Matter, Quantum Science or Physics. Whatever you want to call ***him***, ***her*** or ***it***. The Power is simply **Alive**.

So what if we are just here on an assignment?
Or what if humanity is just an experiment?
And what if all what we say is even true; -Who cares?
We don't call the shots!
Let's just get on with living life, learn, and make the most of it.

CHAPTER 8

LET'S BANG ON! - *At least for a bit*

I've heard about the bang! The Big Bang!! All this banging.

But I don't understand what caused the Bang, to bang!

It bangs out of nothing; I heard that. - But what caused nothing to become something in order to trigger the BANG!! -?

For now, let's just come to a compromise and call it the **God Bang**! I'm just not in the mood for the Banging.

We earthly people have benefited immensely from Science. We have been blessed with some of the most life changing scientific rewards from the kingdom of Science, which have heightened and maximises our planet tremendously to a great extent.

All humans should be forever grateful and indebted to all of our distinguished scientists, who continue to bring great contributions and vital benefits to our world.

But Science doesn't know **everything** as we know!!

In the case of the Banging, Science told us "**how**" but it can't tell us "**why**", not yet.

We should keep our channels open for every possibility, and even look beyond Science.

As spiritual beings we are open to enlightenment, so at all times, our cognitive portals should be open like a receptor, ready to receive and process more information.

We will always be growing and changing at different stages of consciousness; striving without limits and moving with time.

When our earthly mission comes to its close, the bell rings, and the body drops!

But for spiritual people like myself, life doesn't end at the end of the body.

Life lives! That's all life ever knows. The part of life that continues to live is still there.

Call it whatever you like; Spirit, Soul, or divine Self.

The body only borrows life from this energy, and it became the vehicle that takes us around throughout our earthly experience. The vehicle no longer needed when this journey ends.

CHAPTER 9

HAVE YOU MET THE SINNERS? - *Were we are born in sin?*

Born in sin? Oh really! Maybe you were; but I sure was not. -Hell NO!

I was born pure and spotless! Innocent and flawless! No blemish. I can't begin to imagine what wrong would I have done in my mother's womb that the minute I was out, I sinned? - You can rewind that again!

Children are the most innocent souls, purest in love and with the most immaculate of spirit! You will never find a more virtuous, guileless being than that of the newborn soul. When a baby emerges from the womb, the soul of that infant is the ultimate representation of purity, bearing God's stamp of approval all over it.

You know you're in the presence of the highest form of saintliness.

Sadly, we lose our innocence as a consequence of growing up!

David was allocated the authorship for the book of **Psalm**, and in **chapter 51:5** he says, *"Behold, I was shapen in iniquity; and in sin did my mother conceive me."* The text doesn't actually read what is widely interpreted and preached by the church, that we were born in sin and shaped in iniquity. But it is clearly implying more or less the same thing. And with that interpretation, it leaves a lot of people bewildered and duped. They believe they are not worth anything in this world under the watchful eyes of God, and the only way out is if they choose the biblical path.

Almost everywhere we go we can hear preachers beating the drum on this particular scripture; and I'm not sure if they are aware of the harmful impact it has on the lives of innocent misled people.

We have people like Paul, in **Romans 3: 10-12** who made it worse when he said, *"There is none righteous."* In other words, no one is good; there is nothing good in us. We were born in sin and become filthy and worthless and there is nothing about us that is good. They have been drumming this in our heads from God was a boy. I'm sure they expect us to feel less than human.

That word "Sinner" carries a very foul stigma in our society. It breeds scorn and cunning discriminations without anyone even noticing. It's like a mild prejudicial insult.

It's clearly stating that you are transgressing against a divine law, by committing immoral acts.

And these immoralities can be as simple as, thinking something malicious or having a lustful desire in your heart, without even effectuating the thought in any practical form.

You can get done for just having natural affection. You are not permitted to find someone affectionately attractive in your heart. It is a sin to be harbouring these type feelings inside of you, said the Bible.

I wonder how they go about choosing their partners in the church if they're not allowed to find each other sexually attractive and desirous, which begins in the heart!

The scripture says in **Matthew 5:28** that, *"But I say unto you, That whosoever looketh on a woman to lust after her hath committed adultery with her already in his heart."*

Their thinking capacity has been restricted by God according to the church, that they are never to lust at anytime at the opposite sex in their heart.

Ummm! *–I must be the dumbest person reading this.*

And can you believe that highly educated people swallow this <u>bull-dust</u> -?

These distorted beliefs only hold us back! They are misrepresented, and no God would assign authority to such nonsense.

It's hindering our free will of thinking, and suppressing our spiritual growth.

If we just look around at the ingenious creation of our universe, it should become clear, that texts like these undermine God's intelligence. How could God then be so clever, and yet dictate these irrational things to someone, to write in a book? God would have made sure that they got it right. -I would *fire* him!

God didn't lay these instructions down in the first place.

These biblical propagandas are dreadfully detrimental, and it affects our quality of life as human beings. They have been carefully implanted and drenched in our mental psyche by deception.

When a so-called sinner like myself meets a so-called holy child of God, we're often looked at through a different pair of lens. The minute they work out that you are non-religious, you feel that swirling in your belly.

You're overwhelmed with the sensation of a person speaking and looking down at you through rose coloured-tinted glasses, so you can rest assure that you won't be getting a cup of tea or a friendly face.

Once you're being observed as a sinner, you are then seen as less important. You've possibly been sneered at a thousand times, masked under a counterfeit smile.

The reason I know this, is because I have come across it quite a lot whenever I am around some hardcore Jesus special forces.

<u>*What is "sinning" in their terms*</u> -?

Human errors, lying, cheating, criminal acts that are punishable by law -?

Do they mean the daily mistakes we make and learn from -?

I thought these were normal human behaviour from the beginning of time, which formed the factors of evolution in the developing man!

We transform; we mature! -It's part of the human make up of self-renewal.

Throughout the ages, these features and characteristics help to enhance the growth of man. This is how human beings strive and learn, develop and change.

What is **sin** -?

I should think that before God made us, God already knew what to expect from the imperfect man. I think that's why we were given the function of the conscience within us, to differentiate right from wrong; so we know when our emotion pierces the stomach, something is questionable and not quite right.

So if we choose the hasty or egoistic option, life teaches us that we have chosen the wrong way. It has never been in the ego or haste. It is always found in calm and silence. All the positives, sit in love and light only.

Erase this notion of *guilt and shame*, and the ridiculous belief that you are a sinner and set your mind free. As the legendary Bob Marley says, "***none but ourselves can free our minds***".

We are evolving and living exactly the way the divine source required it to be. The only thing we need, is to use our conscience in the act of good for all humanity and all that co-exist on the planet.

It's a very degrading term in my view! Utterly disrespectful!

Stop calling me a sinner, because you do what I do too.

I only speak of it the way I see it. And as our dear friend Danielle would say,

"What's on my lung rolls off my tongue."

In the mind of the religious believer, a sinner is not a winner in any shape or form. Hence you are fitted with a doom vest, and without realising, they pull the shutters down on you.

But you can take the vest off and push the shutters back up. It's really up to you!

I guarantee you God will smile: -

CHAPTER 10

THE NEW TESTAMENT HERO - *Apostle Paul*

Most biblical scholars and theologians came to the conclusion unanimously that Paul is the first writer for any material in the New Testament. He supposedly wrote between 50 and 60 AD some where along there. Followed by Mark in around 70 AD, then Matthew, Luke and then John in that order.

I have to say I find Paul grossly annoying. I can't stand the guy! The one thing that gives me comfort in all of this is, is that not one of them might have existed as far as historical facts point.

But I want to base this purely on the New Testament texts, just the way it was written, and focus mainly on the Pauline's writing.

According to the biblical record, Saul who was later given a Greek name Paul was born in Turkey in a place called Tarsus. He was first known to have been on a violent mission, as a savage persecutor to destroy the church following the death of Christ.

But then he passionately embraced it, after experiencing a so-called mysterious encounter with the voice of Jesus on his way to Damascus.

This was said to be the beginning of Paul's pilgrimage, which allegedly gave rise to Christianity becoming a world religion.

A lot of theologians and modern scholars still argue today about the reliability of the account in this story, that it may never have taken place, and I doubt it too.

The book of Acts introduces Paul and tells us a little about him; but this book is full of inconsistencies, as well as the writings in many of the 14 books they attributed to Paul.

Suspicions have always surrounded who really wrote the book of Acts.

Some say it could be Timothy, Some say it could be Titus. Plenty believe that Silas was an eyewitness, so he could have possible wrote it. Others held the belief that it was Paul himself.

But the most general view held by many, is that Luke who was a disciple of Paul, is most likely the Author.

Some of the early church fathers like Jerome, Eusebius, Irenaeus, Origen and a few others all seem to have a vast consensus in their writings that Luke wrote the book of Acts.

Now Paul first showed up in **Acts 7:58** under the character of a young man name Saul, when Stephen was then sentence to stoning by the Jews. Saul was blamed for consenting to Stephen's murder. (**Acts 8:1**) We then go on to learned about his conversion to Christianity in chapter 9, and there the inconsistencies began.

For a while I've been hearing people calling Christianty "Paulianity", and I find it hilarious.

I know there was something dubious about his writings, but then I put them under the lens, and it dawned on me that this man is high-risk.

Paul is the only person in the bible that blurted out some astounding **lies**, and he tells you very clearly that he's lying!

Listen to what he said here, **Romans chapter 3:7**; *"For if the truth of God hath more abounded through my lie unto his glory; why yet am I also judged as a sinner?"*

So in other words Paul is saying that, If God is happy and getting the exaltation, even if I'm telling **lies**, why are you then judging me -?

Or in other words "who are you to be getting upset with me -?

I think he's bonkers!

Go to **2 Corinthians 12:16** and tell me if it›s my head spinning!

Paul says, **"But be it so, I did not burden you: nevertheless, being crafty, I caught you with guile."**

Now you tell me, who in their right mind could trust someone who speaks like this?

Paul wrote that Jesus rose from the dead according to the scriptures and appeared unto Cephas, then to the "*Twelve*" and 500 more people after that. And then he concluded, that last of all he appeared unto him Paul. Well I take it that he was talking in his sleep; because if Jesus appeared unto Paul after he was raised, then it could not have been face to face. Everyone knows that nowhere has it been recorded that Paul ever met Jesus in his lifetime.

But how about the bit that said, he appeared unto Cephas, then unto the "**twelve**". -Which Twelve? Hold on a minute! - I thought Judas hanged himself after he betrayed Jesus.!!! And they did not initiate Matthias as a replacement among the apostles as yet, according to Acts chapter 1. So which Twelve did he appear to? The brother is delusional.

CHAPTER 11

PAUL SAID I DID WARNED YOU – *That I am crafty!*

When Paul preaches and sent out letters as we see it in the bible, he uses this phrase, *"According to my Gospel."* These can be picked up in many parts of his work such as, **"Romans 2:16; Romans 16:25 and 2 Timothy 2:8;**

There maybe many readers who may consider this to be petty!

But the more I unpack Paul's work, is the more I begin to worry. He repeatedly says "According to my Gospel", and I am not sure if I understand what he means.

He emphasizes so many times throughout his texts that he's getting his messages direct from Jesus, or by divine inspiration!

But let us look further at some of the twists.

It appears to be that "Paul's Gospel" is the complete opposite, to that of Jesus' teachings, and it comes under a new title called **Grace**.

Paul talks a lot about the law, which is the Law of Moses laid out in the Torah, that of which the Jewish nation has long acknowledged and abide by.

This is the Hebrew Law! Some of the things include in this law are, obeying of the Commandments, observing the Sabbath and the circumcision of all male.

And God said that no one is to add or take away from the law, according to the scriptures, and that these laws are forever permanent throughout generations.

Jesus made it very clear and distinct in **Matthew 5:17** when he said, *"Think not that I am come to destroy the law, or the prophets: I am not come to destroy, but to fulfil."*

But here is Paul on the scene with a new interpretation of the law, tailored and remodelled under a new found label called Grace or Salvation, despite Jesus' instruction in **Matthew 19:17**, that if anyone wants eternal life, you should keep the commandments.

Here is Paul's version to what Jesus said in **Matthew 5**; *"Christ hath redeemed us from the curse of the law, being made a curse for us: for it is written, Cursed is every one that hangeth on a tree"*, **Galations 3:13.**

Now this is a direct twist to what Jesus said, as we were told. - **So who is this guy** -?

If only he was around today, he would have a huge platform on twitter.

My question is, who should the Christians be following, **Paul** or **Jesus** -?

On top of that he cemented it in **Romans 6:- 14-15;** *"For sin shall not have dominion over you: for ye are not under the law, but under grace. What then? shall we sin, because we are not under the law, but under grace? God forbid"*;

We can see modern day Christianity, hinges heavily on Paul's gospel more than that of Jesus'. This can only be construed as a Grave Deception in the history of Christianity.

One of the Jewish sacred laws is the act of circumcision. Paul changes this as well.

He wrote in **Galatians 5:- 2-3**; *"Behold, I Paul say unto you, that if ye be circumcised, Christ shall profit you nothing. For I testify again to every man that is circumcised, that he is a debtor to do the whole law".*

Hellooo! What the *Foxtrot Uniform Charlie Kilo* is going on -?

And you can see more of these texts all over the Epistles of Paul, in **1 Corinthians 7:18**: **Galatians 6: 12-13**: **Colossians 2:11,** and a lot more.

I just would like to know **who** really is The Boss here -?

My conclusion is; Paul corrupted the scriptures very badly; but ironically it turns out to be helpful indirectly, because it opens up that area in our minds that was closed. We can see the flaws and all the different interfering fingerprints, indented all over the literature. Can you still say that these things were inspired by the Genius, Intelligent, _Can't-Make-Mistake_, Omnipotent God?

They were poorly thought through, these horrible scripts.

Who ever wrote them, clearly didn't done the geometry, before attributed them to a most probable non-existence Paul.

I just love when man makes plans, and God laughs!

CHAPTER 12

NOT ALL GOOD PEOPLE ARE RELIGIOUS

NOT ALL RELIGIOUS PEOPLE ARE GOOD!

Everybody knows this is so true in every walk of life. But perhaps it is mainly because of what we expect of these religious brands.

My mom and my sisters are all Christians, and sometimes I can't stand their annoying behaviour in my little brain. But I realise that it is only because I'm looking at them as Christians, and not as humans behaving like real human beings.

All I can see is this 'tag' called *Child of God* which is their fault, because they have set the bar so high, as if to say, when you see me you should stand in **awe**, because I represent God's bosom friend. In other words, I am The *Child of God* and you **are not**!

And for a lot of folk, this Child of God title really elevates them way above others sadly, and their ego soars!

But being a good person should not mean you have to be part of a religion. It is the ethical motive that begins the *good persons* process.

It means that you have taken time out to push your ego back and begin to follow the path to simply become a better person. It is called enlightenment.

By using the functions of the heart, and the use of the conscience in a particular way, you become enlightened; it's an internal function. You allow yourself to think non-violent and compassionate thoughts. It's when you become selfless instead of selfish.

I think that's very easy to do. It's probably the healthiest spiritual thing we could do for ourselves, which is filling ourselves up with kind thoughts.

How hard can that be, to generate and send out nice energy to everyone and everything; making a situation and yourself feel better; giving your heart permission to smile.

We gain much more benefits from carrying around a light heart, rather than hopping about with the heaviest, full of "sorry-for-me" heart, showing all the pronounced wrinkles on the top of our foreheads.

Nobody likes bad energy, grubby people lingering in our space. Naturally our "good_person" receptors pick up on these things and put up an instinctive rejection, which makes us immediately uneasy around such energies!

When we arouse thoughts of love, kindness and peace and becoming more grounded and centred in our self, we are taking a stroll down the path towards finding our God consciousness.

There are a lot of clean-hearted good people who are religious, and some of them I know will bend the rules of their religion if they have to (at least slightly), to accommodate any good gesture or act of kindness, which may not fit with their religious dogma. But I think they do it because they know that God is not silly, and there's a little silent voice speaking in their heart saying, "Nothing is wrong with that."

Humanity can become better. We can clarify and harmonize all disputes there is, if we want to. We just need to fall in love more with all creation, and do it without prejudice. This relationship is important for universal harmony. Nobody has all the answers; but you must always follow your good intelligence.

We ought to recognize the symptoms for what is holding us back. One of our main setbacks is failing to see the need for material simplicity.

We are all too obsessive in focusing on how to attain and stockpile the planet's wealth! We tend to forget easily that we are going to die, and we are all just **waiting in the queue**!

It really makes me wonder if humans are truly this dumb; the gluttonous behaviour of the majority looks as though, some just want to be the richest person in the cemetery. It's a fake knowledge!

As in Donald Trump's *most famous line*, **"*it's fake news.*"**

We are all staring in a big movie here on earth! We get dropped from the scene as we go along, and get replaced by another act, super quick!

This is one of the things that prevent us from developing our good human self. We will need to get rid of egocentric behaviours and start seeing that we are all one, and none of us owns **Nothing**!

If you can't take up the land that you build your house on, and bring it with you wherever you go, you don't own it. It wasn't yours!

Whether you are religious or not, it doesn't count when it comes to striving to become a better person. That's doing something personally for you.

Maybe you're just trying to understand the noises on the planet, and sailing with the current on the natural order of nature.

We should practise not to just say things that sound good, because that never helps people. It is always better to tell the truth, even if you have to find a *"not-so-hurting"* way to present it.

Simply do what you have to do and don't worry about getting credit for it, because this isn't a contest. We are not here for the "Ego Awards", or to win arguments. We are just here to share, and help each other.

But as I say this, I know by writing this book, it puts me in that position where I will be called dreadful unending names, probably deemed as the ***dark blasphemer***.

But guess what! I have some news for you, and it's in the next chapter.

Learn to live simply and use what you have and be contented. Always maintain a spiritual practice in your life and stay in connection with the divine, and become friendly with it.

CHAPTER 13

<u>I REALLY CAN'T WAIT TO DIE</u> - *A little poem called "Death!*

I am so inquisitive, I am not shy; I want to know the truth, I really can't wait to die.

Mommy, daddy, sister, uncle, Aunt - I don't know how you use that word "**Cant**".

Ok.! Take a breath! Let me introduce to you **Death.!**

Greetings! I am Death.
I am here to draw your last breath.
I am not prejudice of whom I select,
Just doing my job which is a hectic project.

I take the waiter, I take the chef,
I take the dunce and the very intellect,
The queen in her glory, she will be next,
I take the dumb, the blind and the deaf.

Even new born babies whether he or she,
Once I get the order, they are here with me,
The rich, the poor no matter how loud they plea,
I even take Christ and hang him on a tree.

I am that part of life that definitely guarantee,
Doesn't matter who you are, you shall be with me,
I am not that bad, though a lot of you may disagree,
But the day when I claim you, of course you will
see... - **The End!**

CHAPTER 14

THE GOOD BOOK! - *The Good What -?*

The bible is the most outstanding literature ever put together for many people. Others describe it as the greatest book ever sold and the greatest **Lie** ever told, which I agree.

Personally, this is the worst book ever written; largely because of the psychological damage it has done and is still doing. It carries a very penetrable effect, mainly on vulnerable faint-hearted individuals who are often packed with fear.

The minute you come in contact and fall in love with it. CLICK **BOOOM!!** You're pinned.

When you first read this book, it brings you to an inviting emotional place. It starts because you have problems, and this book is telling you that it has all the answers for these; so you dig even more deeper. Soon and very soon, your newfound love turns into an **addiction**.

When I was about 14 years old I spent a couple of hours in a police station in Spanish town. I got into a petty punch-up with a classmate of mine by the steel factory. A police officer was nearby, and to cut a long story short, we both ended up in a little room at the station; more like a waiting area than a cell.

I got real shaky and scared, as it dawned on me that I might be in trouble, but mainly thinking how am I going to explain this to my dad.

I found myself starting to talk sternly from my grieving heart saying, *"God, if you get me out of this place, I will start serving you and put away all bad things."*

I was convinced totally to the core, knowing I meant everything that I said. Sticking to the principle that when I make a promise, I do my endeavour best not to break it - (worse, I promised **God**).

It was no more than about 20 minutes after I said this, I saw this lady I knew from my community walking in to the police station, so I shouted at her "Miss Lynn," and she came by the tiny window, and I started to pour my heart out to her. And again cutting the story short, within 15 minutes of telling Miss Lynn, I was walking out of the police station uncharged.

This was where my religious journey began, and I went on to honour the promise I made to **God!**

Now looking back, and then forward to my age of 52, we have to be rational when it comes to choosing our path to life and monitoring what we feed our brain. When I was 14, my brain was still like mushy peas. I was still in the crib.

So how does this work!

You first get hooked into this endearing invitation, which holds a promise in it. The promise is to solve all your problems.

Now depending how intuitive you are, you may quickly discover, there is an underlying basis of fear emanating from these rules, which you have to follow in order to be qualified for this promise. The principal charge that you are given is that you got to believe the scriptures.

When you sign up and begin your religious excursion, that fear becomes much more real. It becomes your truth, and you can't leave the club because you will be eaten up by your guilt and fear.

It takes hold of your mind like a drug, and you become too afraid even to contemplate leaving.

I mean, even if you physically walk away from the church and backslide, you're still intoxicated with Jesus.

Now this is the disturbing menace that I have identified within this so-called Good Book, among other things. When you're in it, you're completely blindfolded. You never sift through anything!

Everything biblical that you read or hear, your brain interprets as **truth**! After all everything comes from the mouth of God.

You also donate heavily, liberally giving to this organisation the moment you become a member. The Bible instructs that you should give one-tenth of what you earn in life to the organisation.

So as a believer, whether you're earning or not earning enough, you try your best to find something to give. And you give, because you were promised, that if you give this to God, you would be blessed ten-fold.

So your programed brain just sits comfortably in that mode.

You're here everyday looking for the blessings, which cannot arrive and never come.

When in reality, that's just one of the many **Fat lies** told to us in the book. It definitely works for them, but never for you.

Even after you step away from the church and look back at the many years of contributions you've made, you just sadly have to face the delusory fact, that this was a ***Trick & Treat!*** -You treated them to trick you.

You gave them a physical blessing in exchange for a spiritual one, but you got ripped off, because you weren't connecting the dots.

You were only **fastened** there because of your fear. It is called **Fear**-mongering!

Fear of the concept of being burnt in hell fire; a pictured that sticks in your mind.

The minute you wake up from that delusion, you immediately become free! And that's one truth they told us in the bible; one of my favourite verse; *"And you shall know the **truth** and the **truth** shall set you free."*

The moment you believed that your Jesus was nailed to a cross; in that very moment, they've psychologically nailed you as well.

You are plugged into a system functioned by guilt and terror, which is why it can become so depressive and grim, when the reality proves the opposite. It's like your prayers have not been answered.

If there's one thing I don't get about religion, it doesn't allow you to have fun with the world. You don't have freedom of your **self**.

And when it's vaccinated into your system, it becomes normal.

The best thing you can ever do as a Christian, is to **backslide**, if you truly want to be *saved*. The quicker you do this, on a serious level, the better chances it will be for the recovery process of your sanity.

CHAPTER 15

SHOW ME A STONE OR EVEN A BONE - *Just show me something!*

For many years I pondered about the biblical characters mentioned in the bible. I wonder where their tombs are today? No shrine built for Jesus' mother Mary, no tomb for daddy Joseph anywhere; no burial site for Mary Magdalene or none of the twelve disciples that allegedly walked with Jesus; except for that of the Catholic Claim made about Apostle Peter, that he had died in Rome, and hence they built the Vatican church on top of his grave in order to fulfil the so-called words of Jesus in **Matthew 16:- 18-19** "*And I say also unto thee, That thou art Peter, and upon this rock I will build my church; and the gates of hell shall not prevail against it. And I will give unto thee the keys of the kingdom of heaven: and whatsoever thou shalt bind on earth shall be bound in heaven: and whatsoever thou shalt loose on earth shall be loosed in heaven*".

The Vatican adopted this part of the scripture and established it as the fundamental code of the papacy. So by building the church on what they claim to be Peter's grave, Jesus automatically gave them the keys to the kingdom of heaven; and so, we have the papacy today known to us as the Vicar of Christ, which means *"Earthly representative of Christ."*

And here is the most interesting bit; they ordained the so-called dead body of Peter as their First Pope. – <u>*Apostle Pope Peter*</u>!

Now considering this was only 2000 years ago when all this was supposed to have happened, which in hindsight is not that long ago, comparing to the history of our world; and yet there is still no bones, no authentic tombs; no monuments or significant memorial locations that exist anywhere today of any of these biblical personalities.

But lets go back to at least 3500 years, and unearth some hard facts that we can verify and see with our eyes today in Egypt, over in The Valley of the Kings, by the west bank of the Nile.

There are 63 tombs in that area displaying rock solid physical evidence of Egyptian Pharaohs mummified bones, all lying in their tombs this very moment, in this very second, on this very day.

Bones and remains of the embalmed bodies of Tutankhamun, Amenhotep, Ramses III, Hatshepsut, Akhenaton, Thutmose III, Seti I, and many many more, are all there in the Royal burial ground, buried with their earthly treasures in their tombs right now!

These tombs were built as far back as 1539 BC, and I wouldn't be the least surprised if they turned out dating them much earlier too. Everything is preserved and engraved inside and outside of these tombs and on the lids. The brilliant thing about the Egyptians is that they wrote everything in Stone. So the confirmation is staring at you in the face, **set in stone**.

Towards the end of the eighteenth century until now, The Valley of the Kings has become an Archaeological scientific excavation site and numerous documentaries have been, and continue to be made.

Just break the mould! - Smash it!

What helped me break away from this mould, and what I would firmly recommend to anyone who find themselves searching for answers while serving in the church, would be to research BC history on religion.

Find out what the religious world was like, before Jesus came on the scene. That's a perfect starting point and a real eye opener for your pursuit. In everything you do, you should always have a searching eye, and do your research. Never take anyone's word for totality. Just do your research!

I can name at least 15 or more Saviour Christ having all the attributes like Jesus; all born from a virgin, walked with disciples, walked on water, worked miracles, was crucified and raised from the dead in the same 3 days, just like him.

The only difference is that they all happened before Jesus; some predated him as far back as 3000 BC. Here are some of the mythological gods for you to zoom in on, in your research!

-Horus, Attis, Hari Krishna, Mithra, Dionysus, Heracles, Buddha, Zoroaster, Huitzilopochtli, Erechtheus, Qi, Hatshepsut, Tammuz, Adonis, Ra, Plato, Romulus; the list goes on.

No doubt they are legendary figures, but the important thing to look at is, these myths were all prominent and trendy in those times and preceded the New Testaments account by far; dated back to hundreds and thousands of years before the Common Era, which proves that Jesus' story is just a copy of these mythological figures.

The Jesus account is quite similar, especially to that of Horus and Mithra.

There's not one compelling piece of evidence, which proves that God had ever sent human deities to the earth, for the purpose of saving souls.

Throughout human history, there are always legends and miracles known among man in all cultures and civilisations, and it continues to be recycled and retold down the line by our ancestors.

The thing is, they are all still around today, doing the same things that ancient man use to do back in those days, except that their **names** have now been changed.

We still have the conventional Magician; but there are some brand new lingos on the scene, like Psychic; Obeah Man; Astrologers; Mediums; Voo-doo; Witchcraft, Seance and loads more of other modern day slangs.

And at some point in most of our lives, we either hear about or have seen some jaw-dropping experience of todays Magicians performing astounding tricks in front of our eyes. Today we see our magicians turning water into Prosecco, by hovering their hands over it; and it leaves us wondering how the flying floating fox did they do that?

It was called Miracles then, but today it is Magic, Obeah and Clairvoyance. It's the same principle, only under a different label.

This so-called Good Book is supposed to be about the history of the world and its events. But arguably, as I said, there is not one shred of tangible evidence to show where God dictated even a tiny part of this literature to any human being.

And mainly so, because a lot of it is too ludicrous and no God would be so unskilled and way off the mark with some of these idiotic ideologies written in these texts.

This book was clearly devised by men who are always on the natural quest to understand the creation of the universe and the mind of God. In today's world, that quest is called Scientific Evolution.

For me, this so-called Good Book is a **lethal** document. If you find yourself swimming in the deep, and confused or trapped like I was; do yourself a well-deserved favour! -**Just leave**.! Walk out in confidence. There is no wicked God who will be coming after you to punish you.

You're only closing the door on a well-marinated history of Lies and Myths.

Close it! Just **leave**! –Do a Brexit.

Chapter 16

THE FEAR OF GOD IS THE BEGINNING OF WISDOM

What wisdom? Why are you scaring me -?

<u>*How did they do the arithmetic for this -?*</u>

In all the time I spent in church I never comprehended this precept, that if we fear God, we will become Wise! -***Psalm 111:10, Proverb 1:7, Proverb 9:10.***

What is this Godly fear promotion business all about? I still can't fathom how they even managed to pull this one off and get so many airplays. They even enticed seemingly bright-educated graduates on their books, when it is clearly hogwash.

What type of melody are they hearing in the word "fear" that I'm not hearing?

I just wish someone could sensibly explain, how they worked out that the spirit of fear gives birth to wisdom.

We all know what fear symbolizes and the negative overtone that it conveys. The elements of fear are boundless. It is worry, panic, agitation, nervousness, distress, horror, anxiety, unease and unrest: all of these constitute to fear. So what type of mixed messages are these texts transmitting?

The scripture says, throughout our life here on earth, we should live every part of it in **fear** and especially if you are a person who calls on God.

It is quite unfortunate that these words are actually written in the Bible. Read it in **1 peter 1:17**; *"And if ye call on the Father, who without respect of persons judgeth according to every man's work, pass the time of your **sojourning** here in **fear**".*

Are you serious! How much more nonsense must we produce from this -?

I cannot even imagine love and fear blending much in the same settings, without one cancelling out the other.

Listen to the conflicting disparity written in this sacred text. The bible is now telling us that fear and love cannot mix together, because love is perfect.

Read and listen in **1 John 4:18**; *"There is **no** fear in **love**; but perfect love casts out fear, because fear involves torment. But he who fears has not been made **perfect in love**."*

Based upon that, I think we should do the opposite of fear. We who believe in a God should only love, and not fear the

God of our universe. God doesn't want anyone to fear the power; Love is a much stronger force to distribute, than the energy of fear; and it is far more effective.

God already knows that humans are frail and can't even stand up to the wind and the sea, much less the awesome power that creates them. God doesn't need to threaten mankind or intimidate the fragile feeble man.

It seems to be more like a tool for use in the favour of the church, rather than a charge from God.

First they set down rules that we should follow and then tell us that these are inspired policies from God; adding, that God is very jealous and angry and he even kills children and dumb animals; so you must worship this God in trembling fear.

But here is the evasive craft that comes in straight after; "The **Fear** of the lord is the beginning of wisdom." **Proverb 9:10**!

Hence, there is **no** other way that you can acquire wisdom unless you begin here, with this **Fear**! - And that's the peg that bolts you down right there.

Now we can get you to obey anything we want. Your adrenaline has now infused with trembling **Fear**! - It's a clear headshot from the sniper.

CHAPTER 17

CAN I SELL YOU JESUS -? *Not sure if I would buy him from you*

Here is a man who is the Central pillar to one of the biggest religious movements on the planet; Christianity is a dominant force in our culture! Every Sunday people have large gatherings all over the world to hear or give a story about this man. We should now use our best efforts to understand this story. It is one that gains momentum very quickly and spreads rapidly. It has been sold to many of us time and time again. The name of the man is **Jesus**.

From what we know about Jesus, it is really not a lot. Sadly most of us can only tell the story by the way it was told to us in the bible. Unfortunately there is no demonstrative evidence from the actual time of Jesus to support this historical man, except for what we know which comes from the four Gospels in the New Testament, and these were written decades after the event they described.

Other sources would be, compositions from early church fathers, who all started their writings after the four Gospels; almost a hundred years following the event.

The huge decades of gaps between the crucifixion and the writings of the early bishops, indicates that none of them were eyewitnesses to the incident.

It is then fair for one to say, that the framework of their script would most probably derived from their own personal persuasive viewpoint.

Up until today, there is still no enthralling archaeological evidence. No factual material to convince billions of hearts that this historical man "**Jesus**" had ever lived.

And it makes no sense to hold these literatures as reliable data. We're just hopping on the band waggon because it's exciting and popular! - One fool, turn many Fool**s**.

Looking at the closest chronological records we have of Jesus, which is what we get from the four Gospels; and to be fair, they are overflowing with colourful contradictions right through. They also contain some exact copied and paste style similarities, which prompts suspicion about the authenticity of the work.

According to the scriptures, we know he was from Palestine, born as the carpenter's son. He had his baptismal ritual done by his cousin John; he then enters the preparation for his ministry, and his developmental process began.

We know next, that he started preaching and became the subject of the Roman Empire, which was the world Super Power at the time.

The depiction of Jesus was that, he came as an agent of God who was critical of the law, and took the law in his own hands and became the most controversial figure, of that era.

He was condemned and stood trial and was given the death sentence by crucifixion.

But what else do we know about this iconic Jesus? Where do we start to search for the historical person?

There could be a possibility that there was no Nazareth according to wide spread belief. Some hold the view that the town may never have existed, basing their facts on the premise that it was never mentioned in the Hebrew writings, nor by Josephus nor in the Talmud, and these are all eras before, and shortly after Jesus. -But I don't know. I am still unpacking.

The way that it unfolds, it seems like up to a century AD after the crucifixion, nobody seemed to clutch the event as a great significance, or even seeming to be concerned about it at the time; considering it was a fulfilment of the Hebrew prophecy and one of the most crucial points in the Jewish history.

The first manuscript of this Saviour figure event came when Rome published the Josephus "Jewish Antiquities" in 93CE. Josephus was born 4 years after Jesus died, so he didn't know

Jesus. He would have grown up in the Pauline eruption, in the time when the disciples were going around preaching.

I am not banishing the likelihood of a "rebel" Jesus activist, who was perhaps speaking his mind and lashing out at the crooked government that was in place at the time; because that's a definite possibility.

I am arguing about the traceable account of the man himself in history "Jesus", who supposedly came here en-route of a virgin birth; he was a miracle working deity, the saviour who died on the cross between two thieves for the sins of humanity. The only thing missing so far is, none of this is conclusive.

What I find bemusing is that, even though a lot of scholars questioned the historicity of Jesus, it appears that many of them still haven't taken into account adequately, the vast amount of substantial evidence they uncovered. Or perhaps they just bypass them, but **why** -?

For instance, the "Christ/***Christos***" title that has been long associated with a number of characters in the Greek Old Testaments (The Septuagint) like in the persons of Saul, David and Solomon. And even though this was prior to the birth of Jesus, It doesn't seem to open up too much in their interest.

We read the Greek account of the their god *Serapis Christus* in the time of Alexander 3rd century BCE, and we have vividly seen the same duplication in the story of the Jesus Christ narrative in the New Testament account. And even the famous picture of Jesus that we know and see today, looks identical to that of *Serapis Christus*. Just type his name into any search engine on the Internet, or go to your history museum and have a look for yourself. This image was introduced 300 years Before Christ by the Pharaoh Ptolemy 1 Soter in Egypt.

So there are definitely qualities that have been adopted from pre-existing deities, and not just Serapis but many others, and these were clearly applied to the personality of Jesus. Too many likenesses of borrowed components are just there looking at you, which cannot be ignored because they are very vital to this Jesus analysis.

This is why it's an on-going struggle to filter through the Truth and the Lie, which always entangle the structure of religion.

In saying that, we know the name "Jesus" might have been a fashionable name before it applied to The Christ. One of the criminals sentence to be killed with Christ, was called "Jesus Barrabas." Also Paul mentioned in **Colossians 4:11** this other Jesus whose surname was Justus. Again it mentioned in the Apocryphal book of Sirach / Ecclesiasticus, which was written around 180 BCE. Its author Joshua Ben Sirach who also was called "Jesus the son of Sirach of Jerusalem." That is because the name "Jesus" is a translation of the Greek word "Joshua", or "Jeshua" which is also a rendition of the Hebrew name Yeshua.

And therefore it is important to know that Joshua in the Old Testament was the successor of Moses, his name was also **Jesus**.

My suspicion is that these New Testament writings maybe just there to be understood only in allegoric terms. Paul talked about two of Abraham's sons in **Galations 4:24**. One of which he had with an Egyptian slave woman and the other with a Jewish free woman; a story that comes across very racist if you ask me. But basically what he was saying is that these two sons were only an allegory, they were really two covenants in reality.

The whole concept of the Jesus story is that it has no logic in it. I think this is one of the worst ideas that someone could have ever come up with.

I still don't get the reason why Jesus had to die for the sins of man; and why did his "Dad" sent him down to earth to be tortured and murdered in order for him to forgive human sins. Couldn't he just forgive his children without requiring a human sacrifice in return? That's a red flag for me.

One more thing I want to clarify here... But... maybe this question has to be directed to the angry God of the bible (not the universal intelligent God)!

Why would God send Jesus on this operation, **knowing** that his son cannot really die, because Jesus has always been an immortal being according to the scriptures -?

And as we can see, he got up and walked out the grave after three days, so he did not really die.

So, what *yu saying bruv*, did God actually trick us into believing that Jesus' death was to pay the price for our sins?

Because if he died for our sins, then he shouldn't have got back up, because that's the price he came to pay as part of the deal.

If this is not cheating, then they are trying to tell us that God staged the crucifixion!

Yes I know exactly how bizarre it sounds, because I just wrote it...

What I don't exactly know is what to do with Jesus. There are so many beautiful lies told of him. I didn't know that I would see the day when I could say that there was absolutely "**no**" Jesus Christ, and it feels like freedom.

Never in a million years would I have thought that this conviction would come from my mind, considering the religious back ground I once defended and grew up to believe.

There are no verifiable facts to corroborate the Christian writings.

Every attempt of validation submitted by philosophers to date, keep failing the reality test over and over again.

One thing I know is that, our universal intelligent God that created the cosmos would not have done something so nonsensical. I think the story wasn't well thought through, and now the Truth is eventually catching up with the Lie.

When you follow the train of events, it mainly carries a lot of political overtones. No wonder so many Scholars are pointing fingers at the Roman government, holding them answerable for the fabrication of this tale.

I subscribe to that club. – Admission: *FREE*!

Chapter 18

RELIGION – RELIGWRONG *-How would you pronounce it?*

In every culture, race and philosophy, Religion has long played a fundamental role in the life and forefront of human civilisation. It has always been a topic of debate and lots of controversy. The core basis of religion is a belief in a God or gods, although not all religion shares this belief system; for instance, Buddhism is a kind of godless religion. It is more about the way of living their life according to principle, of which they called it Dharma.

However, they all carry the essence of "divinity" which could be a God or even nature, or anything that is deemed to have a sacred element about it.

For a lot of people, religion is a place of comfort, and I can relate to that because I was at that place. The motivation is normally triggered when unanswered questions about life, such as losing loved ones, illnesses, ultimate fear of death, or simply the security of your children. When these fears rocket and hit the "troubled" spot, that's the moment when you turn to this place. It's an escape. It becomes your umbrella for shelter in that desperate hour of need.

And it is because there is always a demand for security within man, like a vacuum that must be filled. This is where Religion steps in and takes advantage of the niche market.

As I have mentioned beforehand, that I had once mounted the podium of religion, championing the cause of my belief; and I know belief is valuable, but it didn't answer my quest for reality!

I am not an Atheist. I firmly hold the belief that there is a God force, higher Supreme intelligence working behind the functioning of this marvellous reality.

But for me God is not a word; God is nameless and genderless.

Religion was created from the mind of man, so man gave name to God.

Man sometimes need to take a chill pill; step back and let the process of causation do its job, which is, to gradually unfold the story in front of our eyes, where we learn marvellous things. It always produces the evidence in its own time. Allow it to come to surface in its natural stride! Unmolested!

We are so packed with constant fear, which is why we run to religion for security. Fear is a dreadful thing, but technically religion uses it as their principal channel to lure you into fellowship.

They persistently drip-feed your mind with dense pressure, telling us about damnation and the melting of bones in the lake of fire.

We are constantly reminded that God is going to get even with his unruly disloyal children one day, and burn them unquenchably in this furnace of fire for eternity.

I warned you! The ambush happens so fast; it's like a quick dream. You soon find yourself clapping in church by next week.

It's amazing how God can be so sinister, and yet merciful in the same breath!!

I couldn't bear to see my little pet dog I had, called "Black Mouth", getting burned in a blazing fire and my heart not weeping and ripping out of my stomach with excruciating pain.

Am I more loving than God-?

I have never said this aloud, but when I use to read the bible in my younger days, I always whispered to myself and said, God seems to have a very bad temper! For what satisfaction could God achieve from watching powerless humans roast in a blazing furnace of fire, knowing that we are so feeble and insignificant before this great force?

God can simply send us to bed and we never wake up. None of us! -It's that easy!

I pronounce it **ReligWRONG**!

How about practising the long old-standing religion called "**Love.**" Everybody knows this; we hear it all the time.

But share what we have amongst each other and minimally attach ourselves to material things. Have them in your hands, but keep them away from your heart as much as possible.

We only have a limited time in this experience, so we should never find the material world too attractive, and get too comfortable with it, placing it above humanity.

We should eat, play, laugh and brush shoulder to shoulder with everyone. We are here to mix among every race and culture, without the slightest titchy speck of prejudice.

It is crucial to note, since we were given the name "**human race**", that all humans are then related and belong to this one race. Although we may vary on the outside in different skin colour, it is important to acknowledge that we are only just **One** colour on the inside - **Blood Red**!

And it's essential to keep in mind that everything starts on the inside.

We only need to bring closer, the intellectual understanding of our world. Just like how the zebra which got it stripes, and the leopards given their spots; goats have horns and beards, and they all come in different colours and shapes in the animal kingdom.

In the same way we as human beings come in different colour and shape. We are in a multi-coloured universe where everywhere we look in nature, we see multiple colours all around.

This is the colourful diversified mind of the Divine Mystic.

Of course we can do this humans. I have never seen a racist dog; or a discriminative cat nowhere! We just have to stretch the horizon of our minds beyond what we see on the surface.

We are way advanced in science and technology today. We make weapons that can literally wipe each other off the planet in seconds. Can't we develop a device to "**Love**" one another too -? You never know - Give it a go.

Love is the most important force that functions among us on earth. It's a divine magic! It works all the time and has a very strong magnetic field.

It is also free and easily accessible from the heart.

It's the God within you; and all we need to do, is start tuning in to use it.

Meditation is the best place to start.

Life is far more worthy, than to live it just on the paradox of religion. I'm a billion times more convinced to stay where I am on the platform of Spirituality.

It is the tale of the **truth** and the **lie** for me when they both went out for a swim.

I took the concept from Dr Ray Hagins. When I heard him tell the story, it stuck in my craw for months.

Eventually the truth caught up with the lie and unclothed the lie, and that is what's happening in religion.

I would like to take this moment to summarize the facts I have presented in this publication. It is very clear to me that the world's most popular religion Christianity, is a political construction developed and outspread by the Roman Empire during the 1st century AD.

History shows that all the bishops and early church writers especially Josephus Flavius, all played a fundamental role in the development and amplifying of this doctrinal conviction; sitting under their palm trees and in their sheds writing <u>lies</u>, under the meticulous guidelines of the Roman government.

You have to give the mother of all Christian churches her dues, which is the Catholic Church. Her theology, ethics and liturgy express deeply, and gives oxygen to the successful formation of the Roman Catholicism, and it is still a force to be reckoned with in today's world. It still stands as the pillar of the Christian foundation, no matter what denomination there is.

I personally believe that we are now at that time where reality collided with delusion, and this big block of religious ice is slowly starting to melt.

There is nothing much sweeter than knowledge and knowing the truth. It really sets you free inside.

When found, and you gradually start to understand the energy of the universe; you eventually become ONE within it!

Religion in my view needs to be revised or simply abandoned; it's definitely expired in today's era of technology.

Each time I think about life under religion, I can't help but think about the Avatar, the one who has to be in the middle like a portal, where you have to go through **him** to access **God**? That's what closed it down for me.

The mind-set needs to reset! Thank you very much for reading!

Printed in the United States
By Bookmasters